Against All Odds

The Eddie Storm OAM

Story

Vee Bellamy

Dedication

To all the men and women I had the honour to meet and entertain in Vietnam, who made my life worth living.

To Lisa Gardiner Co-ordinator for The Mandurah Seniors and her staff. Thanks to all the audiences and social groups across Perth and the Peel RegionFor their long time support.

Acknowledgment

With special thanks to The Hon. David Templeman, who is a remarkable man who represented our City of Mandurah for many years.

Janice McGlinn OAM, who first booked me on my return to Mandurah, at the Mandurah Senior Citizens Centre — her support was wonderful.

To Bernard Carney OAM, Director of the City of Perth's Morning Melodies.

To Dawn Yates, Seniors Recreation Council of Western Australia.

To all the various community groups from the Peel Region and Western Australia.

To my fellow entertainers from across Western Australia.

And in memory of the late Max Kay AM, whose encouragement and support helped shape my journey.

Contents

Foreword

Eddie Storm's story is one of resilience, talent, and heart. From his barefoot beginnings in wartime England to becoming a beloved entertainer across two continents, Eddie's journey reminds us that the impossible dream is never out of reach. He has brought music, laughter, and healing to thousands, and it has been my great honour to walk beside him and witness his unwavering devotion to his audience.

This book is a tribute not only to his life but to every soul he has touched with his voice and kindness.

— Vee Bellamy

Chapter 1
Childhood in Plymouth

Eddie Storm, born Edwin Alfred Bellamy on June 3, 1932, was raised during the Great Depression. His family had very little. He would run barefoot to his Granny's pub where, in exchange for a packet of Smith's crisps, he would sing on top of a small table. He sang Vera Lynn's songs like 'We'll Meet Again', bringing joy to locals despite the grim wartime atmosphere. These performances sparked a lifelong passion for music. His granny's care, the echo of bombs, and the love of song laid the foundation for everything that followed.

Chapter 2
The War Years and Evacuation

In 1939, when Eddie was just seven years old, World War two. In 1940, Eddie, his mother, and brother were bombed and buried alive at night. The following morning, we were rescued by the police and neighbours. The trauma left a deep mark on him. Eddie and his brother Raymond were evacuated to St Ives, Cornwall, sometime later Eddie was hospitalised where he had the misfortune to meet and was bullied by the matron, while removing his pyjamas for a bath and was unable to untie the knot in his pyjama bottoms he was forced to wear a girls night gown, he was very shy and said that it was the most humiliating time of his life when his mother visited the hospital - Eddie informed her of his experience and his mother took him home to Plymouth until the end of the war.

Chapter 3

Early Work and the Army

Some humour comes up. At a young age Eddie struggled in school due to shyness and poor eyesight he asked the teacher if he could move to the front of the class, when he was asked why, Eddie said he could not read the blackboard the teacher realized that he had given Eddie the cane for not doing his homework, Eddie became his number one pupil the teacher wrote to Eddie's mother requesting for Eddie to stay for another year in class his mother insisted he leave school because they needed the money. Eddie obtained a job as a butcher's boy. The butcher, unfortunately, had a speech impediment. He handed Eddie a large bowl of mincemeat. Eddie thought that he said, Give it to the fish, in the backyard, as there was a large pool with fish. Eddie promptly threw the mincemeat into the pool. Later, when the butcher asked Eddie where the mincemeat was? Eddie proudly informed him that I gave it to the fish. The butcher's assistant told Eddie that he was told to put the meat in the fridge.

On another occasion, whilst riding his bicycle with a large basket on the front filled with meat delivery customers' orders. One delivery ended with him and the meat crashing into a customer's swimming pool, bicycle, and Eddie. When Eddie returned to the shop dripping wet, he was sacked on the spot. Soon after he got a job as a baker's boy, The bakery consisted of a bakehouse at the back of the shop Eddies job was to skin potatoes and delivering fresh pasties—from the bakehouse to the shop he was given one hour each day for lunch the baker then went for his hourly lunch after several weeks Eddie decided to sneak into the bakehouse and make his own pastie, he knew he could make a pastie and be out before the owner returned. Eddie then made a giant pastie and placed it into the baker's oven. Ten minutes later, the owner returned.

He said that he did not need lunch that day. Forty minutes went by, and the baker asked Eddie if he could smell anything. Eddie shook his head whilst his knees were trembling. In hindsight, he knew that the baker knew what was going on. Another ten minutes went by, and smoke started billowing from the oven. Eddie admitted that he had made a pastie. The baker opened the oven and replied… that is some pastie–Eddie was promptly sacked.

Chapter 4
Boxing and Military Life

At 16, Eddie took up boxing and quickly showed promise. By 18, he had been conscripted into the Army, where he continued to box. His fists did the talking, and he became the champion lightweight of the South West of England. His Army years, though hard, were some of his most formative. Despite hunger and hardship, he found strength in discipline—and discovered a new calling: entertaining. Working as a cook, he often sang for the troops, earning their respect.

Chapter 5
ENTERTAINER

Music followed Eddie, whilst in the Army, he would sing in the canteen during lunchtime, his commanding officer once said Bellamy! Your voice is louder than a bugle. Singing helped lift spirits and gave Eddie a sense of purpose. After completing his service, he knew he wanted to perform. Music had become his lifeline.

The Army gave him the will to become a singer.

He remembered when conscripted into the Army, he was one of 600 new conscripts, all young, we were led into a large hall with a stage, for a concert … someone on stage asked the audience if anyone could perform, no music.

Eddie immediately raised my hand and was invited onto the stage to perform. He recalled a sad song about a young man who fought with his father, packed up his belongings, and kissed his mother goodbye.

Eddie performed the words–I was riding along on a freight train, bound for nobody knows where, for I left home quite early one morning, and my heart is heavy with care, for I quarreled with my dear old father over some wrong that I did. He called me a drunk and a gambler, not fit to be called his son. I cursed and I swore at my father, I told him his words were a lie.

I packed up my clothes in a bundle and went to kiss my mother goodbye. My poor mother broke down sobbing. She said Oh, my son, do not leave your poor mother's heart will be broken, and all through the long years, she'll grieve. I know she'll be there at the windows day after day as I roam, watching and waiting and praying for the boy who will never come home.

Now, my friends, take a wonderful warning: don't break your poor mother's heart.

Stay by her side, cos she needs you, and don't ever drift apart.

The hall erupted in applause -

It was then that Eddie realized that this performance was his destiny. Eddie never ever imagined that his voice, the performance he had used as a boy under his grandmother's watchful eye in the local pub, would follow him into the military. But there it was. Even among the strict drills, he found comfort in song; he would sing to himself on cold mornings and sometimes in the kitchen when he was on duty as Cook.

It didn't take long for people to notice. The lads started asking

Eddie to sing after meals. A familiar tune— "We'll Meet Again," "The White Cliffs of Dover"—. He wasn't trying to be a performer, but in those quiet moments, music became a balm.

He would often think back to hiding under the bed during the air raids, his mother singing to calm us all. That memory stayed with him, and he understood then that music wasn't just entertainment—it was survival.

It gave people hope.

One day, an officer overheard Eddie singing while cleaning up and asked if he would perform at a regimental event. That one invitation led to many more. Eddie was asked to sing at dances, in the mess halls, and even at a few military weddings. They called him" the lad with the voice," and he started to believe in it again—this voice of his that had once earned me a packet of crisps in wartime Plymouth.

Balancing, cooking, and singing weren't always easy, but he felt alive. The boxing gave him strength, the cooking gave him purpose—and the singing, well, it gave him joy.

Chapter 6
Music and the Ted Coleman Orchestra

Back in civilian life, Eddie began singing in local pubs and halls. His effortless listening style and strong baritone voice became a signature. He sang hits by many other performers, including "Tom Jones"—Audiences loved it.

He commenced working in the Davenport Dockyard on the ships. He received an apprenticeship as a shipwright. One of his co-workers advised Ed that he was in a four-piece band and they needed a singer. Recognising Eddie was always singing on the job.

Eddie got the job performing primarily in theatres for bingo players (who only wanted to play bingo). On one occasion, he sang a Frankie Vaughan song, "If I Were A Tower of Strength." The first time he attempted the falsetto note, it sounded like a foghorn. 2000 people in the theatre roared with laughter. Each time he appeared at that theatre...they all yelled - Sing Tower of Strength, whilst everyone was laughing. I was looking for a hole to disappear. I turned to the band to apologise, and they were also laughing. It became my signature song.

Two years with the band performing at   Billy Butland's

Holiday Camp and other venues - Sadly and horrifically, my band leader and his wife were travelling in a friend's car and involved in a head-on collision, killing three people, his wife the only survivor. She was badly injured.

A lady in the previous audience from Bingo, who was the wife of the leader of Plymouth's biggest bands, Ex Marine Officer Ted Coleman, asked Ed if he had a Tuxedo.

Ed replied, "Yes,"

"Mr Coleman said you start in 2 weeks' time."

That gave Ed 2 weeks to purchase a Tuxedo to be part of an Orchestra with a dozen musicians.

Now his only chance was to visit my stepfather, who was a truck driver who looked upon him as his son, who willingly gave him twelve pounds to purchase a Tux. The 16 years with the band were his happiest years, learning song after song. They travelled from Devon to Cornwall to various venues. He had the honour of singing with Matt Munro, a wonderful man, at the Palace Theatre in Plymouth with the same band.

Eddie was singing with the band until his departure for Australia. The Ted Coleman Orchestra gave him the experience and much happiness, which is all part of who he is today.

Chapter 7
Emigrating to Australia

PERTH PERFORMANCES ON OCCASIONS WITH THE
LATE MAX KAY AM.

Eddie and his family emigrated to Perth, Australia, in 1967,
where they had family residing.

To begin with, Eddie acquired a job in the well-known store
Boans of Perth. A job new to him was to keep food on the table by
selling merchandise.

During the winter, whilst working in Boans, an elderly lady
approached and asked Eddie the price of the cheapest blankets. All
we had were heavy blankets, which were far too expensive, and she
could not afford. Eddie saw tears in her eyes, so he abruptly wrapped
up two expensive blankets, pushed them into her arms, and told her
to run. It took Eddie 3 months to pay for the blankets, slipping money
into the till.

In the meantime, Eddie would enter singing comps in the local
pub and win the final, where a lady in the audience told him that her
sister was getting married in Perth Cathedral, and asked Eddie to sing

Ave Maria for the wedding. It took Ed two weeks to learn the Latin version. After he performed, he was offered a job in a nightclub with a band, which Eddie readily accepted. First Club, Flordita Night Club, where he would sing with the band... In those club nights, they invited celebrities to entertain the audience.

That is where Ed met the late Max Kay AM, a great Scottish entertainer who was well known in the nightclubs and across Western Australia. He became Eddie's mentor. Max introduced Eddie to his manager.

Suddenly, Eddie was in demand all over Perth and the nightclub scene and events.

He became known as "The Tom Jones" of Perth, with Delilah, Love Me Tonight, and many other songs.

During this time, Eddie was making a lot more money than working for Boans. Ed became a professional entertainer and received top billing, having the same manager as Max. Eddie was never out of work as a performer.

Eddie was introduced to Perth's top comedian, Don Martin, who managed the Flordita nightclub and was contracted there once a week. Performing top 60s songs, Delilah....Mule Train....Ghost Riders in the Sky and many more.

It did not take long before Eddie became one of Perth's top performers.

One experience Eddie will never forget...We won't name the club for the following reasons: Number 1, the cheques he paid regularly bounced, so Max and I would walk into his freezer and help ourselves to a meal. Clubs mentioned previously were not the clubs that did not pay.

Work went well in Western Australia. He was invited to audition for Vietnam.

Chapter 8

Vietnam Tours 1969- '70 and Transformation.

Whilst performing across Perth, Eddie was invited to audition for the AFOF. 1969 Vietnam AFOF Vietnam. Australian Forces Overseas Fund.

To perform in Vietnam. Ed passed the audition, which was in front of families and friends. Shortly after, Eddie travelled to Vietnam with his band and other entertainers. Eddie remarked that his experience in Vietnam changed his whole life.

The commanding officer in charge befriended Eddie and informed him that most of the concerts were outdoors, young soldiers sitting on the grass around hilltops, and that some of those soldiers were not going to make it. Eddie recalls that for the first time in his life, he forgot to be afraid. At that moment, his life changed from being a singer to an entertainer. He forgot to be afraid of entertaining.

On one occasion in 1969, the party visited a field hospital where young soldiers were terribly injured.

Eddie recalls talking to one young man whose legs had been blown off. He told Eddie that whilst lying in the field, he thought that he was going to die. He then said that he heard the helicopter, and his words were I knew then that I was going to be safe. Eddie openly wept. He felt humbled to be amongst these heroes.

On another occasion, whilst being entertained by the Vietnamese show outdoors, three helicopters flew overhead at an airbase. Eddie was surprised to see all the airmen giving them applause. Eddie thought it was humorous seeing airmen applauding the helicopters.

He asked one airman why they were applauding the helicopters. He explained that these were the guys who went into the jungles to rescue their troops, the troops who were injured, and, sadly, bringing some brave heroes back in body bags.

On one occasion, Eddie placed a towel over his head as he did not want the troops to see him crying. On another occasion, whilst performing, an alert sounded, and the Concert party was taken to a trench whilst all the sounds of the missiles went on. Shortly after, they went back to finish their concert.

Eddie openly embraced all the troops and sang his heart out to the repaw of those young men and women.

Eddie returned to Perth, and he then completed two tours of Vietnam. Continued his appearances at various nightclubs and hotels.

Chapter 9

Rise to Fame in Perth and Melbourne

When Eddie returned to Perth, he was no longer just a singer—he was a seasoned performer. His shows were polished, charismatic, and powerful. He began performing solo across all major venues and nightclubs. His fame grew, and he earned the nickname 'The Tom Jones" of Perth. Audiences filled every venue to see him perform.

In 1971 whilst singing in a club called the Nanking – (see clip in photos,) Eddie was approached by a Manager of Commodore Motels Eastern States with a contract to appear in Melbourne at various Commodore hotels on a three month contract Mr Kevin Kelly - who became a very dear friend decided that Ed should stay with Commodore Hotels and agreed that Eddie could appear at Nightclubs and other venues around Victoria Eddie recalls going to Melbourne for 3 months and staying for 26 years, returning to Perth to perform at different nightclubs. The LaTenda management invited Ed back to tour a series of clubs in Perth.

One of his highlights in 1971 was winning Australia's New Faces out of Melbourne, singing The Impossible Dream, appearing also on the Penthouse Television show, entertaining, and a series of other television performances.

Appearing at the Myer Music Bowl, which was called People in the Park, with other celebrities.

During his travels throughout Victoria, Ed appeared with Normie Rowe on The Tonight Show. Ed travelled and performed throughout Victoria and Sydney, entertaining at the Sydney Leagues Clubs and various other venues, including Tasmania, where he met a man who became one of his dearest friends, Gordon Clark, who owned the Tullah Hotel, who booked me on many occasions to perform. He performed for several football clubs across Tasmania. Queenstown, Davenport, among many others. The Sydney to Hobart race was performed whilst the yachts were coming in.

He was invited to perform at the well-known Swagman Restaurant at Ferntree Gully, where he performed on a regular basis to a six-hundred-seater restaurant, accompanied by a full band, dancers, and considered a top venue.

In 1985, Eddie was invited to entertain in Perth, to perform in a nightclub called the Godfather, where he met his wife. She sold her publishing business and returned to Melbourne in 1993. When they returned to Perth.

Chapter 10
Community Work and Legacy.

We settled in Mandurah, Perth, where Eddie met the Manager of The Mandurah Seniors Centre, Jan McGlinn OAM, who booked Eddie on numerous occasions to perform at the Seniors Centre, until she retired. Jan brought back memories of Eddie's early years in Perth - when she booked him at many venues. Jan was awarded the Order of Australia for her community work. Eddie is proud to have received the OAM in 2016

Arriving here in Perth without a band, He quickly arranged backing music to appear at various events across Western Australia. The events included the Seniors Expo at the Performing Arts Centre...The Aged Care Games. Crown Perth for The Seniors Ball. Villa Carlotta Tours. Perth City Town Hall. Council's various events are ongoing today, where he concentrates on Care Homes and other events - cabaret shows at Peel Thunder and the Raafa Meadow-Springs—various Sixties Events with his colleagues.

Clem Croft, Kelly Green, Brenton Fosdike, Paul Ewing, Wayne Pride, Moira Scott, Bill Blaine, the Chantelle Sisters, Glenys and Joan, Peter Harries OAM, Ray Van Ross, who also appeared in our Vietnam show here in Mandurah, Dennis Bird, and his 12-piece Hobby Band he has performed with these wonderful entertainers over the years upon his return.

We value our association with the present staff and management at the Mandurah Seniors Centre, who recently awarded Eddie and Vee with a life membership at the centre. Eddie is looking forward to entertaining there in October with Kelly Green and Jenny Wren for a special event.

Thank you to Dawn Yates, Martin, and the team from the Seniors Recreation Council of Western Australia, who have supported Eddie's work over the years. He looks forward to working with them soon for the Aged Care Games.

A very special thank you to David Templeman for supporting Eddie and recommending him for the very special award, The Order of Australia, whom he considers a wonderful friend. Thank you, David, for your wonderful service over many years as our member of parliament and Minister for the Arts.

His friend Bernard Carney OAM from the Perth City Town Hall, who manages their morning Melodies, has supported Eddie over the years.

Thank you all.

Vee Bellamy

In closing, at 93 years old, Eddie recently suffered a heart attack. He will perform as long as he possibly can. He loves people!

Chapter 11
Onward Back to WA

Eddie became a fixture in senior centres, aged care homes, and fundraisers. From the Mandurah Seniors Centre to Perth's Morning Melodies, he brought joy wherever he went. His performances often ended in standing ovations and emotional thanks. He received Life Membership honours and performed alongside other great entertainers at charity shows.

Chapter 12
Still Performing

Even at 93, Eddie continues to perform. From the Aged Care Games to the International Day of Older Persons, his schedule remains active. He says, 'The most important part of being an entertainer is making people happy.' Eddie's voice still resonates like melted chocolate, reminding audiences that joy, music, and memory never grow old.

Honours and Recognition

In 2016, Eddie was awarded the Order of Australia Medal, nominated by the Hon. David Templeman. He also received thanks from the late Queen Elizabeth II. Eddie has a Life Membership with the City of Mandurah Seniors Centre, where he and Vee Bellamy were honoured for their years of service.

Eddie also received the Vietnam Medal for his performances during the war, where he brought joy and comfort to troops and the wounded.

Eddie and Vee receiving an award for Life Membership, Mandurah Seniors Centre, for their Community contributions

Eddie Storm OAM receiving the Order of Australia at Government House, 2016.

Eddie with Soprano Gwenda Uren performing All I Ask Of You from The Phantom of the Opera. Gwenda often performs with Eddie.

Vietnam Medal and Order of Australia medal

1The Governor of Western Australia presented Edde with the honour of The Order of Australia.

Media and Public Appearances

Eddie appeared on 'Penthouse', Mary Hardy's racing program, and was featured in 'Camaraderie Vietnam' and 'Know Your Nation'. His story is archived by the Vietnam Veterans Association and available on YouTube for future generations.

Featured in the archives of the Vietnam War Memorial, entertaining the troops, 1969- 1970.

The Seniors Expo at Mandurah Performing Arts Centre.

Eddie has clips on YouTube covering several Appearances.

Legacy and Media Links

- Know Your Nation: https://youtu.be/LinkToEddieVideo
- Official Website: www.eddiestorm.com

https://youtu.be/WuLW6L6frPo?si=y6J8rY9hEBDi8XQZ

https://youtu.be/jZkp7ct581I?feature=shared

https://youtu.be/qtBeQJe_ca0?si=ffJoMsx_lrGpvXhb

Vee Bellamy

Photo Gallery

Concert all entertainers on stage for a fund raiser The Way We Were Mandurah Senior Citizens Centre

Dawn Yates on the left, pictured with MLA Robyn Clark from Pinjarra, Jan McGlinn from The Seniors Recreation Council, Aged Care Games

Eddie appears at Bedingfeld Care Home with George Boyer on Piano.

Eddie in Plymouth, England, age 18 years, with his Grandparents

Eddie is performing at an Aged Care Facility for his peers in

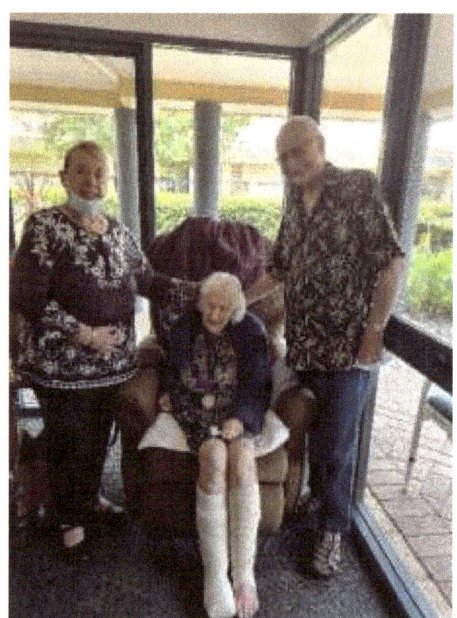

Eddie is performing for a special 103 birthday for the late Jean James a wonderful friend.

Eddie taken in Melbourne 1970s With the Band Something Special at the Village Green

Eddie pictured with the late Max Kay AM from Perth his mentor from his early days.

Vee Bellamy

Eddie's 90th with his colleagues who entertained him on this big day at the RAAFA Mandurah

The Hon David Templeman pictured with Eddie Storm following his award The Order Of Australia

Publicity relating to Eddie's performances

Publicity relating to Eddie's performances

Publicity relating to Eddie's performance

Soprano 93-year-old Gwenda Uren performing on stage with Eddie at Perth City Town Hall.

The popular Nanking Restaurant Perth Manager, sorry to lose Eddie

Two legends together, Peter Harries OAM, with Eddie Storm OAM, enjoying time together

Upcoming show for the International Day of our Elders.

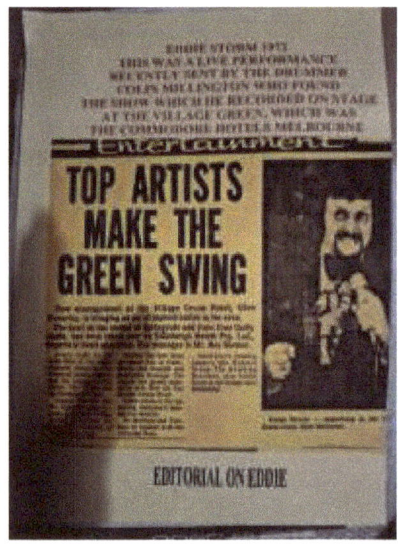

EDDIE PERFORMS VILLAGE GREEN MELBOURNE 1970s

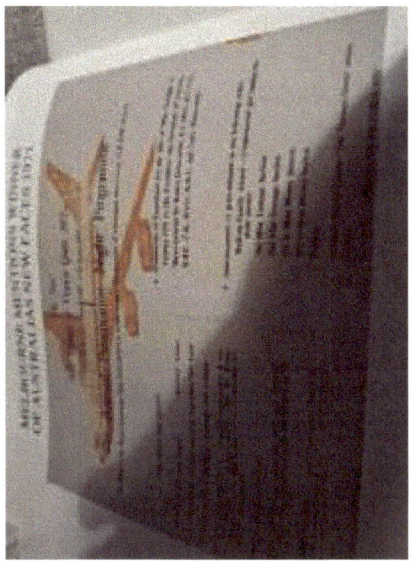

Performing Special Function as Winner of Australia's New Faces 1971

Eddie performed at The Mandurah Performing Arts Centre in 1998 for The Seniors Expo.

Eddie, age 7 years in England with brother Raymond

Eddie and Vee at a special function in 2005

Eddie following stage show George Boyer Kelly Green and Eddie Storm

VIETNAM 2ND TOUR 1970

Eddie performing a fashion show in 1974 for Charity.

Local Mandurah Newspaper editorial

1969 Off to Vietnam, Eddie and his band 1

www.ingramcontent.com/pod-product-compliance
Lightning Source LLC
Chambersburg PA
CBHW051336120626
46547CB00016B/2572